A TALE OF
Two Kitties

Taj and Bodhi

— John Ryan —

Copyright © 2014 by John Ryan

First Edition – March 2014

ISBN

978-1-4602-1853-2 (Paperback)

978-1-4602-1854-9 (eBook)

All rights reserved.

No part of this book may be reproduced or transmitted in any form by any means, electronic or mechanical, including photocopying and recording, or by any information storage or retrieval system, without permission from the publisher and author, except for brief passages for purposes of review.

Book cover design: Weldon Hiebert, John Ryan and Helen Schreider

Produced by:

FriesenPress

Suite 300 – 852 Fort Street

Victoria, BC, Canada V8W 1H8

www.friesenpress.com

Distributed to the trade by The Ingram Book Company

Contents

Acknowledgements iv

Dedication v

Introduction vi

Preface viii

Chapter 1 1

Chapter 2 12

Chapter 3 24

By way of conclusion 51

Photo Gallery of Taj and Bodhi 54

About the Author 83

Other books by John Ryan 85

Acknowledgements

This book evolved from the story told to me by Helen Schreider, a gifted raconteur – a story about her two fascinating feline companions, Taj and Bodhi. The title of the book was a further flash of her insight, and the photographs, which are so crucial to the story, have been a joint effort—hers and mine.

After I completed the manuscript, Helen offered many helpful suggestions for which I am grateful; if it had not been for her, there would have been no such book, so to her I am deeply indebted.

I also wish to express my appreciation and gratitude to cartographer Weldon Hiebert, my colleague at the University of Winnipeg. His technical expertise enabled us to design the cover of the book, and he expertly enhanced a number of photos within the book. I am also thankful to Ryan Givoli for his technical assistance in the early stages.

I extend sincere recognition and profound thanks to Tia Davidson, Publishing Consultant, Renée Layberry, Manuscript Editor, and Author Account Manager, Christoph Koniczek—at FriesenPress—for their combined effort and professional assistance in seeing this project come to fruition.

However, the ones chiefly responsible for this tale are none other than Taj and Bodhi themselves.

Dedication

This book is lovingly dedicated to Helen Schreider and her two dear companions, Taj and Bodhi, and in memory of Zia.

Introduction

I have the feeling that Charles Dickens wouldn't mind me pilfering part of the title of his famous book, *A Tale of Two Cities*—after all, he once said, "What greater gift than the love of a cat?"

Actually, as I've already mentioned, it is Helen Schreider who suggested this title. Helen, of course, is the one who shares her home with Taj and Bodhi, and she figures prominently in the story.

How Taj and Bodhi came to live with Helen is almost miraculous – the difference of a few moments, in both their cases, would have meant that Helen would have never gotten either of them and they would never be together. For this reason alone, *A Tale of Two Kitties* is a story worth telling.

Helen has adapted her lifestyle as an artist to accommodate the needs and pleasures of her two feline companions; in turn, Taj and Bodhi have enriched her life and have brought her much happiness. In her home these two cats have been free to develop their unique personalities, and in the way Helen has freedom in her home, so do these two kitties.

Let me now tell you their story.

Taj **Bodhi**

Helen

Although Taj and Bodhi treat Helen as their equal, they grudgingly admit that she has some special talents and abilities—for example, she is uniquely able to prepare their food and serve it in an appetizing manner, opens and closes house doors and the patio gate for them, regularly cleans out their "Augean Stable," lavishes them with big "licks" using a curry comb and brush, and lovingly dries them off if they should get caught in the rain. She is faithfully available for reassurance and comfort whenever they need it – and above all, they have her love always.

Preface

Taj and Bodhi are two majestic felines, proud and dignified. They appear to be brothers, but they aren't; however, their striking similarity suggests a family relationship. Taj was born in the early spring of 1998, and Bodhi in the winter or spring of 2005. Although Bodhi is now somewhat bigger than Taj, he doesn't challenge Taj's status as the elder.

They live with Helen in a lovely adobe-style home in Santa Fe, New Mexico. Helen is an artist, and their sleeping baskets are in Helen's studio, although they often sleep wherever they please, in any part of the house—especially on her bed, whether she is there or not.

All three are the best of companions, and as far as Bodhi and Taj are concerned, Helen is their equal. But truth be told, they defer to her when it's time for them to eat, or when they want in or out of the house. At these times, they let her know that her special abilities are required, and they make such requests with a slight meow or a little rub.

The story of these two kitties keeps unfolding; every day and every night, they either engage in new adventures or relive previous ones as new encounters. If they are out, they always return so smug and satisfied, but they never tell Helen where they have been or what they were up to. Bodhi, in particular, is the most adventurous, sometimes not returning till late at night. At these times, Helen often sits up waiting for him, wondering where he has gone. While she waits, she sends him messages to be careful, encouraging him to return home safely and soon. And then he suddenly appears, with an expression that says, "Oh, hi Mom! You're still up?"

Out of the many stories that could be told, let us begin with how Bodhi came to live with Taj and Helen.

Chapter 1
Once upon a time, a kitten appeared . . .

One morning, in the late summer of 2005, Helen was startled to see a visitor prancing along towards her on the adobe wall that surrounds her patio. Most astonishing was that this visitor was an almost-duplicate image of Taj—just as if it were Taj as a big kitten! Being on the wall at Helen's height, he brazenly smelled her nose, tilted his head sidewise, and then curled up as coy as could be. He seemed to say, "Hi . . . is it OK to visit?"

Helen stroked him, told him how lovely he was, and that he was welcome. He purred a big, loud purr for a little guy—but before she could tell him about Taj, he suddenly decided he should head home. And as quickly as he appeared, he was gone.

The next day, he was back—but this time, he jumped off the wall, walked across the patio, and peered into the dining room through the patio screen door. Taj was sprawled out on the floor when he suddenly saw this near-mirror-image of himself, with its nose pressed up against the screen.

Taj was a big mature cat; he was seven years old at that time and was in his prime. He considered himself to be the master of the entire residential compound; no cat dared to challenge him, and if one should appear, a single hiss from Taj would settle the matter, leaving him to regally patrol the neighbourhood. And now, suddenly, this impudent little duffer was peering at him through the patio screen, without the slightest concern or fear.

To Helen's amazement, Taj calmly walked up to this little apparition; through the screen door, the two cats smelled one another. As Taj sat back and looked, the young intruder rolled over on his back, exposed his vulnerable belly, and in effect said, "I am no threat to you, and I realize this is your territory."

Plate 1-1. Taj and Bodhi at their first meeting through the screen door. They must have been astounded to see mirror images of themselves; there was keen interest, and no animosity.

Hoping she read the signs correctly, Helen let Taj out into the patio . . . but with a bit of apprehension. By this time, the kitten had stretched out alongside a big green Chinese ceramic planter and, without any fear, just gazed at Taj. It was a friendly look of interest, and perhaps of admiration. Taj was somewhat perplexed, and with his fur a bit puffed up, he slowly approached the little visitor for a closer look.

And that is how Taj and Bodhi met.

To her great joy, Helen witnessed a transformation in Taj. Instead of turfing out the little intruder, as he ordinarily would have done, Taj allowed him to stay. They smelled one another cautiously, then Taj lay down in the shade and watched as his new friend carefully examined everything in the patio. Up to this very day, one of Bodhi's favourite places to lie is beside the big green Chinese planter.

Shortly after their first encounter, Helen discovered that the little one's name was Bodhi* and that he lived at the home of Charlene and Bruce, which was two houses away and connected by the adobe wall. Helen told them that Bodhi had established a friendship with her Taj, and while they were away at work all day, Bodhi would be spending a good deal of his time with his new friend.

---

* He was named after the Bodhi Tree in Bodh Gaya, India, where Buddha attained his enlightenment.

Plate 1-2. At their first meeting in the patio, Taj, a bit ruffled-up, seemed to be saying, "Who are you, and what are you doing here?" By the innocent look on Bodhi's face, his reply may have been, "I'm just visiting. You have a nice place here. Let's be friends. I won't be any trouble."

Plate 1-3. "This is such a neat place! Any chance of me living here?"

Plate 1-4. "No matter what, I'll be coming by every day to visit."

Plate 1-5. And so they became friends—and in no time at all, they were on Helen's bed together.

Plate 1-6. Throughout the fall, Bodhi came by every day. Here, while waiting for Taj, he was having a drink from the bird bath. In the meantime, Taj kept an eye on Bodhi from the image Helen painted of him on the patio wall.

Plate 1-7. "Bye Taj—we had fun, but now I'm heading home."

Plate 1-8. The new playmates, big Taj and little Bodhi. Note the length of Bodhi's tail—eventually he grew into it!

Plate 1-9. The two sleepy compañeros on Helen's studio couch.

For the rest of the summer, Bodhi was a regular visitor, and the two cats romped and played with each other. Every once in a while, Taj would assert himself and remind the young fellow to mind his manners and to remember who was Number One. Bodhi respected this and was quite content to be friends without being too pushy.

Time passed, and Bodhi enjoyed naps in Helen's house, even on the same couch as Taj. Taj was still a bit gruff, but seemed to enjoy Bodhi's company.

As the days shortened, cool weather descended on Santa Fe, and eventually brought snow. Thus Bodhi spent more and more time in Helen's home. One evening, Bruce phoned Helen to ask if she knew where Bodhi was. It was quite late, and Helen had forgotten to send him home. Bruce had been looking for him and was quite annoyed. He then instructed her to not allow Bodhi into her home—Bodhi was *their* cat, and he had to know where his home was.

Poor Bodhi—the next day, Helen wouldn't let him in, and he didn't know why he was suddenly being punished. He sat out in the cold, watching Taj lounge comfortably in the warm house. What an awful dilemma! Helen felt dreadful, as it was just the beginning of winter. But the very next day, Bodhi resolved the problem on his own terms.

Helen was working in her upstairs studio when suddenly she heard scratching on the glass panel of the balcony door—there was Bodhi out on the balcony! How could he have gotten onto a second-floor balcony? She immediately let him in, comforted him, and let him stay in the warmth of the house. But the mystery remained: There seemed to be no way that he could have gotten up there, but somehow he did. The next day he did it again, even though it was snowing.

On the third day, Helen, from a secluded part of her patio, watched and waited for Bodhi at his usual hour to appear. Sure enough, he came running along the wall, but then turned to follow the wall that led directly to the house. He then jumped from the wall onto an aspen tree in her neighbour's patio. He climbed a few feet up the tree, and from there he jumped onto a drain (or a *canale*) that leads from the base of the neighbour's second-floor balcony. From the canale, he leaped straight up about three and a half feet to get to the top of the balcony wall. Once there, he ran around the corner on the surrounding wall, and to Helen's total disbelief, he jumped at an angle over an open space to land about seven feet down onto the lower end of the sloping roof of Helen's sunroom. From there, he raced across the glass panels of her sunroof and leaped up almost four feet at an angle across an open space onto the wall of Helen's balcony. And of course from there, he simply jumped onto the floor of the balcony and proceeded to scratch at her balcony door to be let in.

This complicated procedure required considerable imagination, ingenuity, daring, and an amazing ability to jump. It was genuine problem-solving because it involved a seven-step process—and some jumps were extremely perilous. From the neighbour's balcony, there was a drop of at least sixteen feet to the ground, if he should miss or slip off the edge of the sunroom roof. He perfected this manoeuvre, and continues to do it till this day if he is out late at night, and if Helen has her patio door closed. At such times, she leaves her balcony door open with a light on so he is able to see his route.*

Helen phoned Charlene and Bruce to tell them there was no way for her to stop him from getting into her house by way of this trapeze artist procedure. They laughed and agreed that Bodhi had won. Helen agreed to let him out early so he could get to his home in time for supper and to spend the night with "his parents." Even though Helen would let him in through the patio door, sometimes he would come in through his special overhead route, just for the fun of it. If she were downstairs, Helen would be alerted to his escapade by the big thump as he landed on the roof of her sunroom. She would then run upstairs to open up the balcony door to let him in.

And so the winter passed. But in the early spring, Helen found out that Bruce and Charlene had sold their home and were about to move to a different location in Santa Fe. She was crestfallen that they would take Bodhi away. She was also worried that maybe in their new location they might not be able to have a cat—if that were the case, what would happen to Bodhi?

She decided she would write them a note and wish them well in their new home; in this note, she would mention that if for some reason Bruce and Charlene could not keep Bodhi, she would be prepared to give him a home with Taj, since Bodhi and Taj had formed such a bond. However, before she wrote the note, Bruce and Charlene moved, and took Bodhi with them. Helen was heartbroken that she had procrastinated; now it was too late.

Helen was beside herself, and it appeared that Taj was as well. When Bodhi didn't come by to visit, Taj started going out to look for him. Every morning, he demanded to be let out immediately, and didn't want his breakfast. He would then jump up on the wall and go down to Bodhi's home. Sometime later he would return, looking forlorn and dragging his tail. Usually he carried his tail aloft and always looked bright and alert, but not after Bodhi was gone. He became morose and would mope around the house, and if he heard the slightest noise out in the patio, he'd be at a window looking out to see if his buddy had returned.

---

* Almost all the stages of Bodhi's incredible journey to the second-floor balcony are presented in the photo gallery in the last section of the book.

After a few days—and in desperation—Helen decided to write the note with the hope that her letter would be forwarded to their new address. The next day, while checking their mailbox, she discovered that her letter had not been forwarded. She then posted a note for Larry, the letter carrier, to come and see her. When he came she told him what had happened and wondered why her letter hadn't been forwarded. It turned out that they had not left a forwarding address, so he left the letter with Helen and told her that as soon as he had an address, he would contact her.

A few minutes after he left, he suddenly returned, knocked on her door, and said she'd be having a visitor soon. And then a car drove up—it was Charlene! As luck would have it, as soon as the letter carrier left Helen's house, he noticed that a car had driven up to the mailboxes; it was Charlene, and she had come to pick up her mail. He told her that Helen had a letter for her, and so she came to pick it up.

On greeting her, Helen asked about Bodhi.

"Oh, it's so terrible!" Charlene replied. "Our new home is in the outskirts of the city and our neighbours immediately told us not to let Bodhi out. There are coyotes and bears in the area, and any cat or dog that's let out will be gone in no time—so we've kept Bodhi in the house, and he's been driving us crazy! My brother in Cincinnati is prepared to take him, but it's just breaking my heart to put him in a carrying case and send him off on the plane, all alone. I've got all his travel documents, but this is such a terrible thing to do." At this point, tears welled up in her eyes.

Helen then asked her to read the letter that she had in her hand. Once she read Helen's words, Charlene fairly shouted, "What? You would take him? That's wonderful!" and she embraced Helen warmly.

Helen asked, "So where is Bodhi?"

"He's in his carrying case in the car," was Charlene's joyful reply. "Actually, I was on the way to the airport. I can hardly believe this! If I hadn't stopped to check on my mail, I'd have shipped him off to my brother in another hour or so. I'll go get him!"

Once in the house, she let him out of the carrying case, and Bodhi immediately recognized where he was. Helen called out, "Taj! Taj! Come here, come here . . . look who's here!" As Taj came down the stairs, he was startled to see Bodhi. They slowly walked up to one another, smelled noses, went outside where they kept smelling each another, and then ran into the nearby park. There they just lay down and looked at one other for some time. Then they wandered off. The two boys were back together again!

And that is how Bodhi came to live permanently with Taj and Helen—through the wonder of serendipity, and a truly last-minute and fortuitous course of events.

Plate 1-10. Once they were reunited, they kept smelling each another, perhaps with disbelief that they were together again.

Plate 1-11. Afterwards, they went for a walk in the nearby park.

Chapter 2
And Taj has his story . . .

Just before Christmas of 1998, Helen's beloved Zia died suddenly of an enlarged heart, although he was still quite young. It was all so unexpected, and Helen was devastated. A few days later, a friend asked Helen to accompany her to the Santa Fe Humane Society where she was to pick up a Maine Coon cat. Helen, in mourning for Zia, did not want to go, but the friend was insistent, so reluctantly and sadly Helen went with her. What made this so poignant is that Helen had gotten Zia from this very same shelter.

At the Humane Society, there was a small cat room with rows of cages. As her friend was being handed the promised Maine Coon cat, Helen turned away with tears in her eyes. But then she saw in the very next cage the face of a good-sized white and amber kitten. It was pressed up against the wires of the cage, and with its outstretched paw it was trying to touch Helen. Helen could hardly believe it—the kitten looked like a small version of Zia, but with shorter fur! Helen exclaimed, "Look! I swear it's a reincarnation of Zia!" And it was meowing pathetically as it looked at Helen.

Despite her heartache over Zia's loss, this was such an uncanny coincidence; it caused Helen to think that somehow Zia had guided her here to comfort her. She could not turn away from such an omen, and she asked to have the door opened so she could hold this young cat. Like Zia, this was a male. He had a strikingly beautiful face; his fur was white with flashes of amber at the sides and forehead. His big eyes were locked on hers while he tried to nestle in her bosom, and he held on to her, seemingly for dear life.

All of this was just too much to ignore, so Helen made an instant decision to adopt this little bundle of life and joy. By bringing him into her life, it would not in any way lessen the place in her heart for Zia; this new fellow would just be an addition to her family and would help her to deal with the loss of Zia—and with Zia's blessing, it seemed.

The kitten was so dazzling white that it reminded Helen of the Taj Mahal, so she named him *Taj*, thinking that someday, if she got another cat, she'd call it *Mahal*. As it turned out, her second cat was already named—Bodhi—with a name out of India as well!

Plate 2-1. One of Helen's first photos of little Taj in her home. Here he watched a raging snowstorm from Helen's studio window.

Plate 2-2. In those first few days, Taj was fascinated with the flowers in Helen's studio; it was as if he had never seen flowers before.

Plate 2-3. Taj quickly established the couch in Helen's studio as his favourite place to nap.

Plate 2-4. While preparing New Year's dinner, Helen wasn't able to keep Taj off the counter. He was determined to watch her, but to keep him at bay she placed a Balinese carving in his way.

Plate 2-5. Little Taj... "Is it OK for me to be here?"

It took days for the little fellow to check out every nook and cranny in Helen's home. He was particularly comfortable with all the places and things that carried Zia's scent, and these became his favourite places. For Helen, it was a joy to see her young Taj become so completely at home and relaxed.

Before Bodhi appeared on the scene, Helen was very protective of Taj and would allow him to go out only in her patio, under her watchful eye. Occasionally he would jump the gate, and Helen would go out in hot pursuit to bring him back. However, Taj was not totally deprived of the outdoors; he learned to walk on a leash, and Helen took him out every day for long walks throughout the entire neighbourhood.

Plate 2-6. "I know I shouldn't jump on the kitchen counter, but I just had to check out these birds."

Plate 2-7. When he got his own bed, Taj loved to sleep with his cuddly toys.

Plate 2-8. In this regal stance, Taj showed every indication that Helen's home was now his home. Strangely, in this photo, he looks much bigger than he actually was at the time.

A couple of months later, Helen and Taj visited me in Winnipeg, Canada. Taj didn't mind being in a see-through cloth carrying case, and there wasn't a murmur out of him as he sat under her seat on the aircraft. Unfortunately, the two adult cats in my home, Zephyr and Spice, were very antagonistic to Taj. Poor Taj could not figure out why they didn't like him, and tried his best to become friends with them. This was tragic for us to see, but my older cats were very protective of their home and would not accept Taj. This may have had an adverse effect on Taj, because afterwards he rejected all other cats—with the only exception being Bodhi.

Plate 2-9. Taj in Winnipeg at the Leo Mol Garden in Assiniboine Park. Several passers-by commented on his dignified, majestic appearance.

Taj's return trip to Santa Fe was by car, and he immediately became a superb traveller, unlike most other cats. He enjoyed sitting on a specially built-up platform between the two front seats. From this position, he could easily see all around him, and loved to watch the passing countryside. He seemed to detect possible oncoming dangers. As the car approached the large Canadian Customs buildings, Taj immediately dove under the seat and stayed there without a sound until the inspection was over. Although he had all his travel documents, these weren't necessary since no cat was to be seen by the customs officer. Once on the road again, he peered out to check if the coast was clear, and then got back on his observation seat.

This was a long, three-day, 1500-mile drive (2500 km), but Taj took it in stride. At one point, he had to be sneaked into a motel that discriminated against four-legged guests. He seemed to be aware of his unwanted presence, so he hid under the bed. Great consternation occurred in the morning because he couldn't be found; he had wedged himself into a space under the bed where it took considerable time and effort to find him.

Once home, Taj immediately checked out the entire place to see if everything was in order. For several days he took many long naps to get over his travel fatigue. About a year later, he went on a car trip to Tucson, Arizona. This was only one day of travel, so for Taj this wasn't a big deal. At the Tucson home of Helen's longtime friends, Monique and Jerry, there were two cats as well, Pearl and Lewt, but unlike my Canadian cats, they were intimidated by Taj. By this time, Taj was considerably bigger, so he was quite imposing. To be given such great deference by these smaller Siamese cats seemed to give Taj greater self-esteem, and this experience may very well have made up for the bad treatment he got in Canada.

People used to comment about the lovely lady with the beautiful cat that accompanied her on a leash. It's not often that we see cats being walked on a leash just like a dog, and this intrigued many people. Often they would engage Helen in conversations about how she managed to do this. Once someone said, "Oh, what a lovely cat . . . so majestic he is! How do you keep him so clean?" The reply: "Oh, he is a self-cleaning cat." So Taj had many admirers.

And then through a wonderful series of happenings, Bodhi appeared on the scene—and a new lifestyle evolved for both pussycats . . . and for Helen.

Plate 2-10. Taj's favourite observation post is on top of the wall surrounding the second-floor studio balcony, with the famous brilliant blue Santa Fe sky as the backdrop.

Plate 2-11. Taj keeping a watchful eye on the neighbourhood.

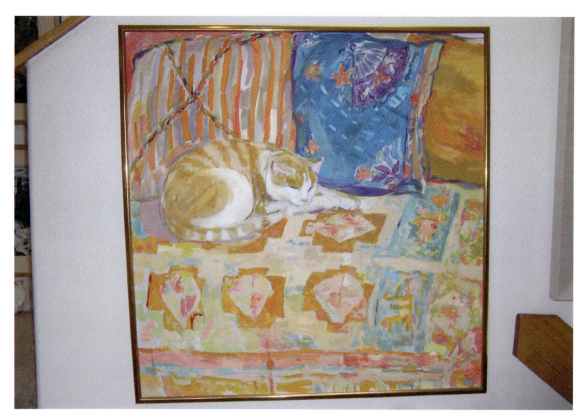

Plate 2-12. Painting of Taj—Helen Schreider, oil on canvas, 36" x 36", 2002.

Plate 2-13. Painting of Zia—Helen Schreider, oil on canvas, 30" x 40", 1995. Zia died of a heart ailment shortly before Taj came into Helen's life. Helen feels that Taj is Zia's gift to her.

Chapter 3
Life with Taj and Bodhi

Bodhi brought about a change in lifestyle for both Helen and Taj. Bodhi is an irrepressible free spirit. From the time he was a kitten, he prowled the entire neighbourhood. Obviously, he is totally fearless of heights, but he seems to be fearless of just about everything. As big trucks rumble by, he just watches from a safe distance, but shows no fear. This is also the case with construction work, street repair, gardeners and their leaf blowers, and the like; he keeps his distance from them, but isn't afraid of their machines, tools or noise. Bodhi is a pussycat that has finely-honed street smarts through skills that he's cultivated since he was a kitten.

And so it was that when Bodhi settled in at his new home, it became very hard for Helen to try to apply a different set of rules for Taj. How could she explain to Taj that although Bodhi was free to go as he wished, Taj could only be allowed out on a leash? As a result, the leash was put away. With some apprehension, Helen opened her patio gate and told Taj that he could go out too, but that he had to be careful! She hoped that somehow, Bodhi would teach Taj some much-needed street smarts. And it seems to have worked. It has now been seven years since Taj has been free to wander, and all has been well.

Plate 3-1. Taj, without a leash, is about to be set free to accompany Bodhi on his adventures, with the admonition, "OK, you can go with Bodhi, but be careful . . . remember where you live, and come back soon!"

Plate 3-2. Taj matured into a truly majestic feline.

Plate 3-3. In the early morning, as Taj re-examined Helen's painting of him on the wall, Bodhi checked out the overall scene. A likeness of Zia rests in the corner where Zia's ashes are buried. Both Taj and Bodhi often sit there, seemingly in communion with Zia.

Plate 3-4. Morning conference in the studio, deciding on the day's activities.

Since Taj had been living with Helen for some years before Bodhi arrived, and had established himself as the head honcho in the neighbourhood, bringing Bodhi into the household was a delicate proposal. In fact, Taj had been with Helen since he had been a big kitten, less than a year old. Largely because of the unusual way that Bodhi suddenly appeared in their patio—not to mention his winsome and non-threatening demeanour—Taj graciously accepted him. No other cat would have dared to do what Bodhi did.

By sheer force of his young personality, Bodhi gained Taj's acceptance, though somewhat begrudgingly. When he was taken away for about a week by Bruce and Charlene, Taj obviously missed him. So in a sense, they had become buddies—and while Taj hadn't been overly friendly, they'd certainly established a camaraderie.

They'll give chase to one another now and then, which is followed by a playful spat. Then it ends as if nothing has happened, and they'll flop down fairly close to one another. One could say that they still have an evolving relationship.

Shortly after Bodhi came to live permanently with Helen and Taj, Helen attended the annual condominium neighbourhood meeting. As she came in, a lady said to her, "Oh, Helen, I hear you've given Bodhi a new home since Charlene and Bruce moved away. He is such a marvellous cat! He used to come to my place for a second breakfast." Another lady said, "Oh, so Bodhi is with you now? You know, he'd come to my place for supper whenever Charlene and Bruce came home late." Indeed, Bodhi had many fans.

Although Bodhi was a lot smaller than Taj when he first appeared, in a couple of years he became bigger than Taj; he now weighs seventeen pounds, compared to Taj at fifteen. In fact, he has an unusual build: he is exceptionally long in body with very long thin legs, and has a very long tail. He loves to stretch out on a sofa with his front legs fully extended. His haunches are high, so this obviously gives him the ability to jump great heights. He has a relatively small head, not unlike a leopard or a cheetah. And strangely, he has small tufts at the ends of his ears, almost like a bobcat. Unlike Taj, who has a regular cat meow, Bodhi very often gives a short, gruff "Mao!" sort of out the side of his mouth, like Humphrey Bogart or some swaggering sailor.

Plate 3-5. Taj: "Sneak up on me, will you! If you don't look out, I'll give you what for . . ."

Plate 3-6. A few moments later, the scene changed; now Bodhi was contemplating, "OK, shall I let him have it, or shall I let him hang in here another day?"

Plate 3-7. Bodhi, giving his legs a good stretch before getting on with the day. Indeed, he has exceptionally long legs, and together with high haunches, it accounts for his phenomenal jumping ability.

Plate 3-8. Bodhi intently studies a couple of pigeons on the sunroof. Note the tufts at the ends of his ears.

Plate 3-9. Taj's moment in the sun.

Now, when it comes to Taj, he is built like a sumo wrestler—solid and somewhat squat, with a big tomcat head . . . someone *not* to mess with. And because of his build and increasing age, he can't jump very high. With some effort, he can still jump over the patio gate from the inside, but he can't jump over it from the outside, since from there it is much higher. Every day, Helen props open the patio gate so Taj can go out easily and come back in again. Bodhi, on the other hand, is like the legendary Superman, and can practically leap tall buildings at a single bound!

When it comes to their colouration—white and amber—they are amazingly similar, as the photos show. Looking down at them as they walk by, it is sometimes hard to tell them apart. However, from the side, they are easily identified because of Bodhi's long legs.

In temperament, they are considerably different. To Helen's dismay, Taj is more reserved and is not as openly affectionate as Bodhi. However, Taj has other ways to show his affection, especially with his soft purr. Bodhi has a loud purr, is exceptionally affectionate, and likes to snuggle up to Helen in bed. It is a wonderful treat for Helen to wake up and find both cats in bed with her—one on each side—so naturally that delays the whole process of waking up and getting on with the day.

Right from the time Taj came to live with Helen, she established a ritual with him regarding eye contact. Whenever he gets hungry, he'll jump on his favourite chair in the kitchen, and then he'll squint at her every now and then. When he does this, Helen will squint back at him; then they will each close their eyes tightly, then slowly open them. At this point, she will ask him if he's hungry, and in response he will quickly blink his eyes; she's come to know that this is his answer in the affirmative. To further confirm his response, he will start to purr with a delicate softness.

Following this little ritual, Helen and Taj engage in another ritual, which they go through almost daily. This is a routine in which Taj selects the tin of food he'd like that particular day. Helen will hold out several tins in her hands, and after Taj studies them for a while, he'll pat one of the tins with his paw. It's Helen's practice to vary the food from day to day, and she has noted that Taj won't select the same type two days in a row—so he must remember the colour of the labels! This is not something Bodhi has picked up, so it's something special just between Taj and Helen.

Plate 3-10. Now, this is a morning that Helen will sleep in. It's hard to disturb well-settled, peaceful pussycats.

Plate 3-11. "Now Taj, which of these tins shall I open for you? Oh, you'd like chicken? Fine, chicken it is . . . ready in a moment."

Taj gets special treatment in another manner: Every morning, his first breakfast is a small helping of warmed baby food. He relishes this, but Bodhi would have nothing to do with it. On occasions when Taj doesn't come down for breakfast when called, he gets further special attention. Helen takes his dish to him while he's still in bed—so he's a pussycat who can claim to get "Bed and Breakfast." Helen still hasn't put up a sign to advertise this service.

When Bodhi can't finish the food on his plate, he very studiously attempts to cover it up by pawing the floor all around the plate. Taj, however, doesn't engage in any such make-believe activities.

Helen has also established an eye ritual with Bodhi, but this occurs only in the morning. She noticed that when he wakes up, usually in his studio basket, he seems hardly able to open up his eyes. He sits upright, very prim and proper, but is obviously very sleepy. Helen will sit on a nearby chair looking at him, and then will close her eyes and slowly open them; Bodhi has picked up on this, and he'll do the same in return. They continue this for a while as a sign of friendship and mutual trust. Finally, he decides it's time to really get up. He then goes through a stretching workout that is marvellous to watch. At first, he stands almost on tiptoes with his four feet close together and arches his back high up, then he'll stretch out his long front legs with his chest almost to the floor but with his rear haunches high up; next, he pushes his head and shoulders up high while his rear legs are stretched out behind to their full length. Helen thinks he should be awarded a diploma for his morning physical workout.

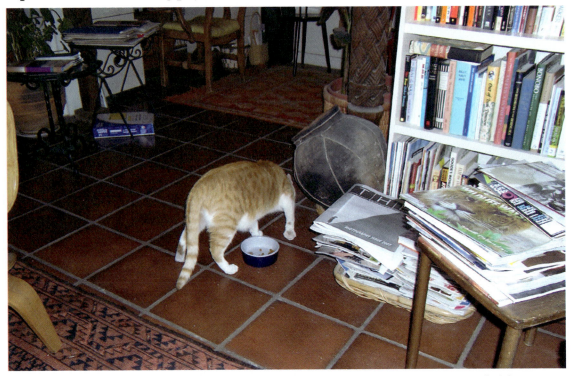

Plate 3-12. Bodhi often attempts to diligently cover up any food he can't finish.

Plate 3-13. This is called "Bed and Breakfast" at Chez Helene.

Plate 3-14. A very sleepy Bodhi . . . to fully wake up, he must first go through an elaborate exercise routine.

    Although Helen doesn't speak fluent "Meow," she has discovered, through her experiences with Taj, Bodhi, and her previous cat Zia, that the nuances of each cat's personality are subtle and revealed largely through their body language. The matter of squinting or blinking their eyes is a sure sign of friendship, but for each cat it happens at different times and under different circumstances. Purring is a profound expression of a cat's state of happiness and well-being. Sometimes she'll find them purring to themselves, especially when they are in the sunshine in a cozy part of her patio, or on the large cushion in the window of her studio. Purring is like a joyful song to be shared with people as a sign of friendship, or just a sign of their sheer joy of living . . . enjoying the sunshine, or perhaps even a sunrise or sunset.

Also, cats have a wide range of meows; it's their melodic, passionate song of deep feeling and expression. Their meows are uttered for different purposes: as a friendly sign of greeting . . . "Hi!", a plea to express their desire for something in particular, an inquiry to see if it's all right to do something, an exclamation that they've found something interesting, or a warning that they're unhappy or feeling provoked.

People who really don't know cats may not realize the extent of their feelings, and their ability to sense joy, happiness, or tension in their surroundings; it is often overlooked that they can experience jealousy, know when to offer comfort and sympathy, and that they have a sense of humour; they can even be bored if there is nothing to play with, or if there isn't anything to do. Yes, cats have personalities, and can be extraverted or shy and retiring. Also, anyone who considers protocol unimportant has never dealt with a cat! Poet T.S. Eliot noted that

Before a Cat will condescend
To treat you as a friend,

you must first provide him with evidence of respect . . .

So this is this, and that is that:
And there's how you address a Cat.

Zia was very sensitive and would be offended whenever Helen left him to go travelling. As soon as she would start to pack, he would watch attentively and would be visibly perturbed. Then, as she was about to leave, he would often hide so she couldn't say goodbye to him. On one occasion when she found him, he turned his head away and would not look at her as she pleaded with him to understand that she would be back. When she returned, it would take several days for him to warm up to her. Although Taj and Bodhi aren't happy to see Helen pack, both want to crawl into her bags to go with her! Upon her homecoming, she is greeted with excited meows and many rubs on her legs, as well as a full baggage check.

Helen has a bit of a problem with Taj in that he seems to exhibit jealousy towards Bodhi now and then. She has to be extra careful to give him lots of attention and reassurance. It's a delicate balancing act for Helen so that she doesn't alienate Bodhi in the course of giving attention to Taj. If Bodhi ever has a stressful day, he will be sure to sleep with her and snuggle up closely.

Both Taj and Bodhi have a sense of humour and playfulness. They love to hide and then jump out and spook one another, and they do this to Helen, too. In launching a pretend attack, they'll crouch close to the ground and wiggle their rear ends just before takeoff. Even as they get older, they still like to play.

A further ritual that Helen has established with both Taj and Bodhi is that as she lets them out her patio door, they will pause momentarily; Helen then runs her hand along their backs, from their heads to the end of the tail. Then she'll say, both to herself and out loud to them, "Now you be careful. Don't wander too far. Don't stay out too long. Remember where you live! And be safe. Come back soon."

The cats seem to enjoy this last contact with her; it's hard to say what it means to them, but it's important to Helen. This little caress is like placing a magic cloak of protection over them to keep them safe from the dangers they might confront. Her big worry is the coyotes at the edge of the residential area. Who knows how far the cats wander? They could easily go into the *piñon*-covered hills and canyons. A coyote and a bear were once seen right in the neighbourhood. And there are other dangers . . . other cats . . . dogs . . . cars . . . the "outside world."

For the real vagabond, Helen has a further admonition: "As for you, Big Bode, no birds! OK?" Often he comes home from his forays not at all hungry, so Helen wonders . . . but there are mice out there as well as birds. However, since everyone knows him in the neighbourhood, he may have a place where he gets a legitimate snack.

Bodhi's sense of problem-solving is quite phenomenal. He has figured out not only how to get up onto the second-floor balcony, but also how to get back down to the ground from there. From Helen's balcony, he jumps onto the projecting drain or the canale at the base of the balcony that is at the side of the house. From there, through the branches of a small tree, he jumps onto the patio wall about four feet below, and then jumps onto the patio. Helen has a photo of him in mid-flight as he descends onto the wall. Incredibly, he sometimes jumps directly from the canale onto the soft ground alongside Helen's house. This is about a seven or eight-foot jump, but he must know that the ground is soft in that area.

Plate 3-15. Bodhi, after jumping on the canale from Helen's balcony wall. Rainwater drains from the balcony floor to the outside by means of the canale.

Plate 3-16. A moment after the previous photo was taken, Bodhi leaped onto the adobe wall below—about four feet down—and from there he jumped into the patio.

Plate 3-17. This is Taj's favourite blanket—the one he grew up with. Every now and then he sucks on it, and has done so from the time he was a little kitten. Perhaps it's because he may have been taken away from his mother prematurely . . . and he still misses his mother.

Plate 3-18. Taj keeping an eye on pigeons from his observation post on the second-storey balcony wall.

Plate 3-19. Taj catching the last rays of sunset on the steps leading to the patio gate.

Plate 3-20. Both Bodhi and Taj love to be brushed and combed.

Stories about these two characters abound. Shortly after Bodhi moved in permanently, Helen still wasn't used to his nocturnal escapades, so he caused her considerable alarm one evening. She had her friend Mary over for dinner, and suddenly realized that it was dark out and that Bodhi had been gone for hours. Intermittently, she would go out on the patio and call him, and then go out on the balcony to call again and clap her hands . . . but Bodhi did not appear. She left the dining room door open to the patio and continued with dinner. Before they knew it, Taj, with a determined look, quickly walked out of the house. Helen tried to call him back, but he was gone—so now Helen started calling for both cats.

About a half-hour later, as they were having dessert, Taj suddenly walked into the house. *Thank goodness, at least one of them is back!* thought Helen. Then, less than a half-minute later, in came Bodhi, looking a bit sheepish. Who's to say that Taj didn't go out to find Bodhi?

One day, Bodhi totally spooked Helen's next-door neighbour and their cat, Jolene. It seemed Bodhi had a crush on Jolene, but she would always run into her home as soon as Bodhi approached. This time, however, Bodhi decided to be more aggressive. In mid-day, Helen's neighbour, Carol, heard a great crash in their bathroom. As she came running up the stairs, Jolene was screaming and hissing in the bathroom doorway. And who was in the bathtub? Bodhi! Beside Bodhi was the screen from the window that Bodhi had pushed in. Bodhi wasn't overly upset—he seemed to be saying, "What's Jolene upset about? I just want us to be friends."

On a day-to-day basis, Taj and Bodhi try to participate in household activities, but sometimes they aren't all that helpful. It can't be said, however, that they don't keep things lively for Helen.

There isn't a closet door that these cats can't open. They feel compelled to do a thorough inspection job every once in a while. The only place they linger is in Helen's bedroom clothes closet, where sometimes she'll find one of them curled up on a chest of drawers, especially if she happened to leave a sweater there. It's more difficult to open cabinet doors, but Bodhi has developed a technique to open an Indonesian antique cabinet in the living room. There is no way of deterring him, so Helen has moved her valuable fragile antique pieces to an upper level, leaving Bodhi free to conduct his investigation without reprimand.

Plate 3-21. In addition to being able to open all closet doors, Bodhi is capable of opening some cabinets, including this Indonesian antique chest. Since there is no deterring him, Helen has removed the fragile antiques from within, so he doesn't have to worry about getting into trouble.

Plate 3-22. "OK, now where are all the interesting things that used to be in here? What did she do with them?"

Plate 3-23. "Taj, what are you doing there?" "Just checking, Mom—everything seems to be OK."

Plate 3-24. "Bodhi! You get yourself out of there! That is a no-no . . . do you understand?"

Plate 3-25. Bodhi: "I'm playing with your pencil. Is that OK, Mom?"

Plate 3-26. Bodhi: "Hey, Mom, look at this interesting bird . . . I think it's that big magpie you warned me about!"

Plate 3-27. As Helen paints in her studio, Bodhi watches what she is doing.

Plate 3-28. Taj loves to relax on the sofa in Helen's studio, where he can watch her as she paints.

Jane, who looks after Helen's house when she is away, very quickly learned that Taj was determined from the very first night that he was going to teach her how to look after him properly. After he had his dinner, and as evening approached, he suddenly started meowing, ran to the stairs, and then ran back. He repeated this and kept looking at her and meowing in a perturbed manner. It was obvious that he wanted her to follow him. Then, as she stood at the bottom of the stairs, he kept calling her from the hallway up above. As soon as she was up the stairs, he called her from the bathroom. What she saw was an empty dish on the floor. He stood in front of it, and in no uncertain terms let her know what she was to do. Indeed, as soon as she filled the dish with dry food, he fondly rubbed her legs and purred to thank her, and then he walked away to his bed. Naturally, the food in the dish was for a midnight snack. Helen confirmed that every night he insists on having his dish filled. There will be no hungry pussycat during the night!

When Helen brings in her travel bags, both cats know immediately this is bad news—she is about to leave them to go on a trip. They watch in consternation as she packs her bags. If she should leave a bag open for even a few minutes, one of them will be snuggled in under her clothes or on top of them when she returns. That night, one or both of them will sleep on top of the bags, once the bags are packed.

As she leaves, she explains to them that Jane will be staying in the house and will look after them. "Grump, grump," they seem to say, "but why are you leaving?" They are extremely fortunate, because Jane loves them and looks after them, indulging all their whims in exactly the way Helen does. On Helen's return, they are both overjoyed! They first check out the bags with long careful sniffs. Then they give her rubs, race around the house a bit, and stay close to her. For certain, they will be in bed with her that night.

Plate 3-29. Bodhi: "You're not going away again, are you?"

    Although Bodhi is usually far more adventurous than Taj, there are some exceptions. For example, Carol, Helen's god-daughter, used to come to visit with her big German Shepherd. Taj would come up close and they would smell noses; Taj would then settle down quite close to the dog, showing no fear whatsoever. On the other hand, if someone should come into the house with a dog, Bodhi immediately does a quick disappearing act—no dogs for him, thank you very much. Helen feels pretty certain that Bodhi has developed this healthy precautionary behaviour because of encounters he may have had with coyotes while out on his nightly adventures.

    In more recent times, when Bodhi decides to stay out very late, Helen has noticed that Taj gets concerned about him. Helen keeps the balcony door open and turns on the overhead light. Taj then jumps up on the balcony wall, sits at the far corner, and carefully scans the surrounding area, listening intently. Helen every now and then goes out there and softly calls for Bodhi; in the meantime, Taj just sits and watches. Helen is rightly concerned about Bodhi because of the coyotes, and often one can hear them howl and yelp during the night. The big mystery is, where does Bodhi go at night, and what does he do in the dark for hours and hours? Sometimes he comes home exhausted and somewhat spooked. What kind of encounters does he have? Fortunately, he has never been in a cat fight, or at least he hasn't come home battle-scarred.

Plate 3-30. "Taj, my dear boy, come on in, it's time to go to bed." "Mom, I'm going to wait a bit longer for Bodhi. Where could he be? I've just heard coyotes howling!"

Taj has learned some bad tricks from Bodhi, and every now and then he too stays out till quite late. Helen is more concerned about him than Bodhi, because he can't jump in the way Bodhi does—and he surely can't run as fast. For Taj, she stays up until he gets home. As for Bodhi, once it's past midnight, she sends him messages to take care and to return home safely, and she'll go to bed. She'll wake up every couple of hours to check on him, and often finds him sleeping comfortably in his basket, or on the bed beside her. She'll then go and shut the balcony door and put the lights out.

Every now and then, Taj wants to wake Helen up at some outrageously early hour. In his younger years, he would jump on a low chest near her bed and proceed to systematically knock over the small framed pictures or the alarm clock. Helen was forced to put these on a higher cabinet, but then he'd jump on her bed and would deliberately step on her hair as he headed for the bedroom window. In more recent times, he settles in partly on her pillow; sometimes after a while, when he wants attention, he will blow gently on her hair! "Taj, what is it you want?" she'll ask. "Breakfast? But it's so early!"

Both Taj and Bodhi have a keen sense of Helen's feelings or if there is anything unusual or untoward in their household. This is most evident at any time that Helen is upset, sad, or not feeling well. Once, after dinner in a restaurant, she was unfortunate enough to come down with food poisoning and became desperately ill. This lasted for three days, and during that entire time, neither cat showed the slightest interest in going outdoors. Bodhi spent almost the entire time on the bed with Helen. Taj took turns at "bed duty" and "house patrol."

Zia's ashes are buried in the corner of Helen's patio garden in the shade of a lovely bower of honeysuckle and jasmine. It is most gratifying for Helen to often see one or both of her dear pussycats nestled nearby, as if in communion with Zia.

Plate 3-31. One day, in trying to follow Bodhi to see where it is that he wanders, we spotted him walking along the top of a coyote fence and then jump on a house roof. Moments later, he jumped off the roof and disappeared—and that was the end of our attempt at surveillance.

Plate 3-32. Often the two of them will keep an eye on the neighbourhood from the second-storey balcony wall.

By way of conclusion

Being an artist or a writer is a solitary profession, carried out quietly and often at home. This makes artists and writers an ideal focus for a cat; in turn, the cat is an ideal companion for them, because it likes to lounge or sleep beside them for hours. This certainly has been true in the case of Helen. She spends much of her time in her studio when not travelling. Bodhi and Taj are almost always with her and seem content to be studio cats.

Their life together may be just another small story in the stories of the world, but it is a true story, with no embellishments—and it is worthy of telling. Both Taj and Bodhi came into Helen's life through fairy-tale serendipity, and it resulted in joy and happiness for the three of them. It's a happy story that should be shared, especially at a time when the world is in such desperate need of happy stories.

While Helen paints, her two companions keep her company in the studio.

Photo Gallery of Taj and Bodhi

Plate G-1. The adobe-style home in Santa Fe, New Mexico, where Helen Schreider lives with her two feline companions, Taj and Bodhi.

Plate G-2. This is the first of a series of photos showing how Bodhi manages to get onto Helen's second-storey balcony. This shows Bodhi at Stage 1 as he proceeds along the adobe wall towards the place where he starts his ascent.

Plate G-3. Bodhi, still at Stage 1, on top of the adobe wall at the point where he begins his series of jumps to get to Helen's second-floor balcony, and then into her studio.

Plate G-4. Bodhi, just at the completion of Stage 2, after leaping on the aspen tree from the adobe wall.

Plate G-5. Bodhi, caught in mid-flight in his jump from the aspen tree onto the canale.

Plate G-6. This is momentary stage 3, up on the canale.

Plate G-7. In this photo, Bodhi has just taken off from the canale and is about to land on top of the balcony wall.

Plate G-8. Now it's Stage 4, up on the neighbour's balcony wall. From there he will jump down about seven feet, at an angle over an open space, to land on the roof of Helen's sunroom.

Plate G-9. Bodhi has just completed Stage 6, the jump up from the sunroom roof onto the second-floor balcony wall. We've never been able to get a photo of him at Stage 5, making the precarious jump from the neighbour's balcony wall down to the sunroom roof.

Plate G-10. On one of his first visits to the house, Bodhi decided to have a little nap. A somewhat perturbed Taj seems to be saying, "Hey, this is my bed!"

Plate G-11. "Oh don't be grumpy . . . Helen said it was OK for me to share the couch with you."

Plate G-12. In one of his visits shortly after they met, Bodhi seems to be telling Taj, "Hey, stop looking so gruff. Get off that chair—let's play and go for a run."

Plate G-13. Taj, as a youngster in his early days before Bodhi appeared on the scene.

Plate G-14. Taj's first experience with fire, shortly after being with Helen.

Plate G-15. As a youngster, Taj used to sleep with his toys.

Plate G-16. Taj in his basket, performing his morning yoga stretch.

Plate G-17. Bodhi, in one of his favourite spots beside the Chinese ceramic planter, the place where he first met Taj.

Plate G-18. Another of Bodhi's favourite relaxation spots, in the shade on the balcony canale, from which he can jump into the patio or into the garden at the front of the house.

Plate G-19. "Mom, your desk is a bit messy. Shall I rearrange a few things for you?"

Plate G-20. "Bodhi, I know you're interested in this, but these are semi-precious stones from fragments of a mosaic in the Middle East—not something to eat."

Plate G-21. "Bodhi! That is not a good idea!"

Plate G-22. "Are you sure it's not a good idea, Mom?"

Plate G-23. OK, Taj . . . what's going on here? Which way is up in this photo?

Plate G-24. Taj indignantly asking, "Who dares to disturb my nap?"

Plate G-25. Sometimes Bodhi uses the top of the Indonesian cabinet as a secret hiding place. Zia had also done this.

Plate G-26. As he's about to engage in a good workout on the scratching post, Taj first starts off with a big yawn.

Plate G-27. Bodhi, after a workout on the scratching post.

Plate G-28. Every now and then Bodhi enjoys the view from this angle, lying flat on his back.

Plate G-29. An ingenious way for Bodhi to have a drink . . . but he hasn't quite figured out how to turn on the tap.

Plate G-30. This is Taj's favourite place to have a drink; it seems to bring out the call of the wild in him.

Plate G-31. Bodhi's favourite watering hole—and as close as possible to his miniature deer companion!

Plate G-32. Bodhi's early morning little game of peek-a-boo from the dining room window.

Plate G-33. "I won't hurt your hat, Mom. I just saw it sitting here."

Plate G-34. Bodhi's safe place of refuge, and a splendid observation post.

Plate G-35 Bodhi, as he is now—big, proud and alert.

Plate G-36. Snow doesn't deter either Taj or Bodhi. They both love to go for a walk in a fresh covering of snow, but on this day, Bodhi was out first.

Plate G-37. Home is the sailor, home from the sea, and home is the pussycat, free as can be. And with a smile on his face!

Plate G-38. With Taj in bed with her, along with a good book and her morning coffee, it sometimes takes Helen a bit of time to get on with her day.

Plate G-39. "Hi, Bodhi, are you telling me my nap time is over? Are you hungry?"

Plate G-40. On this particular day, Helen was doing her taxes, but from the looks of things her two companions didn't find it too taxing. It's on this table that Helen brushes and combs the two boys, which Taj and Bodhi both enjoy.

Plate G-41. Now, did Monique and Bodhi talk of cabbages and kings? What was it they discussed?

Plate G-42. Taj in his usual snug place under the still-life table in Helen's studio. Shown is a painting in process by Helen.

Plate G-43. At a special time in Helen's life, she spent six months painting in Sardinia. (Photo taken by a British Vogue Magazine photographer)

About the Author

Helen Schreider and John Ryan

John Ryan is a retired professor of geography and Senior Scholar at the University of Winnipeg where he taught for thirty-two years. He has a Ph.D. from McGill and taught a wide range of courses; his research and world interests took him on travels to over fifty countries.

His publications include many journal and Internet articles, and chapters in books on geographic, economic and political affairs. His major books include one on the agricultural economy of Manitoba Hutterite colonies and one on the life story and art of his late wife, Judith. He is also the co-author of a significant engineering report on the feasibility of using underwater cable in Lake Winnipeg for high-voltage electricity transmission.

His interest in cats has resulted in two additional books—this one, *A Tale of Two Kitties – Taj and Bodhi,* is the story of the cats of Helen Schreider, an artist, photographer, and a former member of the foreign editorial staff of *National Geographic*. A companion publication, *The Saga of the Three Compañeros – Pantera, Leo and El Tigre,* is the story of John's own cats.

Because of the complexity of life, John and Helen have a L.A.T. relationship ("Living Apart Together") in the way that millions of couples all around the world must do because of certain circumstances.*

John is a Canadian, and his home is in Winnipeg, Manitoba; Helen, an American, has her home in Santa Fe, New Mexico—1,500 miles (2,500 kilometres) apart. They talk to each other by phone every day, and enjoy lengthy visits several times a year, including ocean cruises and other vacations, such as a recent trip to Machu Picchu in Peru and a lengthy visit to China. They alternate their visits so the cats in each home know both Helen and John.

---

* For further information on this, see the following articles online via *The New York Times* and *The London Times*:
http://www.nytimes.com/2006/05/04/garden/04lat.html
http://property.timesonline.co.uk/tol/life_and_style/property/article1779831.ece

Other books by John Ryan

The Saga of the Three Compañeros – Pantera, Leo and El Tigre. Victoria: FriesenPress, 2013.

"Where the wind carries me . . ." The Life and Art of Judith Ryan. Winnipeg: Phoenix House, 1998.

The Agricultural Economy of Manitoba Hutterite Colonies. Toronto: McLelland and Stewart, 1977.

Co-authored engineering report:

David Farlinger, P. Eng., F.E.I.C., Allen MacPhail, P. Eng., John Ryan, Ph.D., Ed Tymofichuk, P. Eng., Paul Wilson, P. Eng. *Potential Use of Submarine or Underground Cables for Long Distance Electricity Transmission in Manitoba – A Post Bipole III Concepts Review* (165 pages). Winnipeg: Manitoba Hydro, 2011.

CPSIA information can be obtained
at www.ICGtesting.com
Printed in the USA
LVIC04n2254300315
432653LV00006B/10